Wealth Must Change Hands

By Dr. D. K. Olukoya

MFM Ministries
Lagos, Nigeria.

Wealth Must Change Hands
1st Printing - March, 1998

ISBN 978-0692546963

All Scripture is from the King James Version

Cover illustration: Sister Shade Olukoya

Published by MFM Ministries
13, Olasimbo Street, off Olumo Road, Onike
P.O. Box 2990, Sabo, Yaba,
Tel: 01-868766, Lagos, Nigeria.
E-Mail: MFMONIKE @rclnig.com

Design, type-seting and printing
MFM Press
13, Olasimbo Street, Onike,
Yaba, Lagos.

CHAPTER ONE

THE RIGHT & WRONG
KINDS OF POVERTY

THE RIGHT KIND OF POVERTY

"Blessed are the poor in spirit: for theirs is the kingdom of heaven" (Matt. 5:3).

The first key to the kingdom that our Lord gave us is poverty.

A lot of people oversimplify poverty by reducing it to a material fact. But someone who is rich in money can be poor in spirit. And someone who is poor in money can be rich in spirit.

There are different kinds of poverty, which does not refer only to wealthy. Come to think of it, as far as material possessions are concerned, we are all poor. The man with ₦1million cannot create one tuber of yam or buy one minute of peace, or keep his soul out of hell.

"Money can buy bed but not sleep."

"Money can buy books but not brain."

"Money can buy pews but not salvation."

"Money can buy houses but not peace."

"Money can buy food but not apetite."

"Money can buy medicines but not health."

"Money can buy spectacles but not sight."

"Money can buy amusement but not happiness."

Ten of the 12 spies sent to Canaan by Moses were poor, for they called themselves grasshoppers. The man with one talent in the Parable of the Talents, was poor. He buried his talent in the ground.

Poverty is a state of mind.

Economic poverty is not a virtue. A person can be poor and greedy. The most miserable poverty is that of soul and body.

It is interesting to note that the first key to God's kingdom is a kind of poverty. What is this poverty? It is:

- The realisation that though we posses all things, without God they are nothing.

- To empty ourselves of ourselves and allow the spirit of God to come into the emptiness.

- To be humble.

- The gate through which we enter God's kingdom.

- The essential quality of being accessible to God.

- To tremble at God's word and allow yourself to be pruned by it.

- To be weak before God.

- To be open to God.

God does not need people who profess to be strong. He prefers working through the poor in spirit, whose poverty makes them receptive to Him. Christ has to empty Himself before God made Him rich.

THE BAD KIND OF POVERTY

One of the purposes of this book is to shed light on the wrong kind of poverty and to expose its roots in the life of people. This message will also guide you on how to break the hold of the evil spirits of poverty.

Even if you are rich, it is advisable to read this booklet for it will help to keep you alert against the invasion of the bad spirits. Whenever these spirits are in operation in a person's life, all his wealth and riches will disappear.

The doctrine that a believer should be poor and suffer from financial insufficiency is a very wrong one. It is not in line with the word of God.

As far as the Bible is concerned, Christians are not supposed to be languishing in poverty. In case you have been programmed to think otherwise, here are some Scriptures to substantiate this point.

Deut. 8:18, says,

"But thou shalt remember the LORD thy God: for it is he that giveth thee power to get wealth, that he may establish his covenant which he sware unto thy fathers, as it is this day."

Job 5:22, says,

"At destruction and famine thou shalt laugh: neither shalt thou be afraid of the beasts of the earth."

That is to say that when other people are suffering from lack and want, the believer should be in plenty and be laughing.

Ps 34:10:

"The young lions do lack, and suffer hunger: but they that seek the LORD shall not want any good thing."

Furthermore, Psalm 37:25, says,

"I have been young, and now am old; yet have I not seen the righteous forsaken, nor his seed begging bread."

Psalm 84:11 says,

"For the LORD God is a sun and shield: the LORD will give grace and glory: no good thing will he withhold from them that walk uprightly."

The New Testament of the Bible confirms the truth of the Old Testament.

2 Cor. 8:9, says,

"For ye know the grace of our Lord Jesus Christ, that, though he was rich, yet for your sakes he became poor, that ye through his poverty might be rich."

The Lord Jesus became poor that we might be rich. That was one of the exchanges that took place at the Cross of Calvary.

3 Jn 1:2, says,

"Beloved, I wish above all things that thou mayest prosper and be in health, even as thy soul prospereth."

So the Bible says we should prosper physically and spiritually. You must prosper in your health and in your soul.

Remember that the same Bible says, "Out of the mouth of two or three witnesses, the truth shall be established." Now we have got many witnesses.

Poverty is a bad thing and I, as a person, have decided to be an enemy of poverty. I have decided long ago that I will not be poor. Some people feel that to be godly is to be poor. This kind of poverty is our enemy and we should fight it with all seriousness.

It is a common knowledge that one of the strongest spirits fighting the blackman is the spirit of poverty, and it is a spirit that we have left unaddressed for too long, so that it has been operating freely in the lives of people, and this has led to all kinds of evil things.

Of the few black people who are rich, only a small percentage got their riches from the Lord. Majority of them are spending the currency notes of hell fire bought with their souls.

Poverty among the black people has produced poor food, poor living conditions and an increased desire for demonic assistance. All those involved in deliverance know that the most stubborn and terrible spirits are found among people who are plagued with poverty. Also, 90 per cent of the children who are possessed come from poor homes.

So, it is really a fact when Jesus said, *"The spirit of the Lord is upon me; He has sent me to preach the gospel to the poor..."* We really need to preach the gospel to the poor in Africa.

The Bible does not say that people should be running after money and forget God. A lot of people make the mistake of thinking that poverty is just the absence of money. It is not exactly so. If you are unable to meet your financial as well as other essential needs that make up a good living, it means that the spirit of poverty is in operation. But the Bible treats poverty as a person, that is as a spirit.

Hence Proverbs 6: 11, says,

"So shall thy poverty come as one that travelleth, and thy want as an armed man."

Here, we see poverty addressed as an armed person.

Again, Proverbs 24:4 says,

"And by knowledge shall the chambers be filled with all precious and pleasant riches."

The person with the spirit of poverty is like the story of Nigeria.

There was a time when this country was very rich, but the spirit of poverty helped her to squander her money. The country has not fully recovered both physically and spiritually from this experience. During 'FESTAC '77', the country invited all sorts of demons from different parts of the world to come and display themselves right here in Nigeria. The country used her oil money to sponsor the demons. Since then, she has not fully recovered and the results are there for all to see.

Poverty is, without doubt, a spirit and we must deal with it seriously.

I preached the gospel to a particular man, who later gave his life to Jesus. After we had prayed, I told him about his problem of financial hardship and how his money had been disappearing without his actually spending it. The man told me, that if I knew that much about him, then I must also be in a position to help him. He admitted that whenever he got his salary and put it in his pocket, it would seem as if there was a hole in it from where the money dropped out. Whenever he puts his hand in his pocket, the money would still be there. All the same, he would not know how he spent that money.

The simple explanation is that the money was removed spiritually. The man was lucky to have been able to notice the bizarre incident, because some people wouldn't even know what was going on. This is the point of poverty in operation.

MAMMON

Good readers of the Bible will remember one demon called Mammon. In Luke 16, for instance, Jesus says that you cannot serve God and Mammon.

Mammon is the devil's salesman. He is the one who sells the devil's charms. Those who want to buy witchcraft spirit, fame and popularity go to him. He is responsible for distributing the spirit of poverty that is attacking the entire human race.

When he notices that people are suffering from the spirit of poverty he has distributed to them, the same Mammon will offer to give them easy money in order to dump their souls in hell fire at the end of the day.

He is the controller of the demons of greed, selfishness and financial failure.

Mammon seems to be giving money to a lot of people, but he does this only after he has afflicted them with the spirit of poverty.

You'll have to bind the demon of Mammon and his weapon, the spirit of poverty.

THE DISADVANTAGES OF POVERTY

▸ It may hinder the growth of the believer.

▸ It may open the door for satan to attack the family.

▸ It may open the door for sicknesses and diseases.

▸ It may be a source of temptation.

▸ It may lead to backsliding.

▸ It is not the promise of God for His children.

▸ It will make evangelism difficult.

▸ It will prevent a believer from giving to God.

▸ It will prevent a believer from receiving that which the Lord has promised.

POVERTY DREAMS

The devil afflicts people with evil spirits through dreams. They are called poverty dreams and should be taken seriously. These dreams come in different ways, for example:

- *If somebody dreams about spending money lavishly, like pasting money in the foreheads of women dancing in the street.*

- *If after receiving some money, you dream of finding yourself in the market, buying things.*

- *When you dream of wearing rags or tattered shoes, walking about barefooted, or you see yourself as a beggar.*

- *If you are a trader, and you see yourself in the dream having unsold wares which you display for sale.*

- *If you dream that your properties are being auctioned in your presence.*

- *If you dream as your pocket is leaking or somebody steals some money from you, or you lose some money and after looking for it, you never find it before you wake up.*

- *If you dream of rats running around your house, whether they are big or small.*

If you have about 700 kilograms of foodstuff in the house and there is only one rat around, it will put the foodstuff to a serious waste. It will not finish the foodstuff immediately, but will be taking it little by little. After some time it will give birth to little ones which will be feeding on it as well. The garri will be reduced until it eventually finishes.

> ### *If you dream of your purse being stolen or you find yourself with counterfeit money.*

If any of these things is happening in your dream, there is need for a serious spiritual warfare.

The devil goes about with the spirit of poverty because he wants people to serve him. He knows that when people are poor they will go and serve evil spirits just to get money. I am yet to see anyone who received money from the devil and has not paid a big price for it. The devil doesn't have any free gift. He operates a primitive trade by barter business. The only free gift we have is from the Lord Jesus Christ, given to us by God. Even if you try, you cannot pay God back for His goodness.

You must recognise also that anything existing in the physical can be blocked or hindered at the spiritual level. Actually, it is the spiritual first, then, the physical. Nothing can happen in the physical, if it has not been decided in the spiritual. So, it's possible that the whole money somebody will make during his entire life can be spiritually removed on the day that he is born: The spirit of poverty will stay in such a life and operate there.

I have seen many people whose names were made popular by musicians who waxed records for them, but who are now terribly poor, because the spirit of poverty has taken its toll on them. Even if the toll does not manifest immediately, it will certainly do so later.

A girl told us what she did to her father's business. She said that whenever her father brought a cheque home, she would take the cheque, put it between her legs and take it to an evil meeting and her father would not know how he spent his money.

We have heard cases of people who buried their father's money in the ground. They were spiritually carried out; they are facts.

SIGNS OF THE ACTIVITIES OF THE SPIRIT OF POVERTY

The following signs show that the spirit of poverty is at work in a life.

- *When somebody is having sufficient income and is still having problems financially.*
- *Inability to keep a regular job.*
- *Inability to eat the normal food others are eating.*

Such people may have been told either medically or otherwise to stop eating certain food items, thereby making them eat only the expensive ones.

- *Inability to control child bearing, and send the children to good schools.*
- *When you are always being duped or regularly attacked by thieves.*
- *When you are surrounded by poverty-stricken relatives and you are the only source of livelihood.*
- *When a man patronizes prostitutes.*
- *When somebody has health problems which require a lot of money.*
- *When you keep registering for the same exam again and again without success.*
- *If you hardly get promotion.*

- *If your properties are frequently destroyed.*

- *Being always in debt.*

Believers should cut down or totally avoid owing people money, especially those who know it may be difficult for them to pay.

How to get out of debt

- Stop borrowing.

- Sell items not being used, i.e., use what you have to get what you need.

- Do things yourself when possible instead of paying for them.

- Prayerfully, set goals for paying off debts.

- Secure a job or a better job, prayerfully.

- Saturate your life with the Scriptures.

- Bind the spirit of debt.

- Do not withhold repayment of debt once you have some money.

- Give to God violently.

- Say 'No' to the things you really don't need.

- Stand against gambling .

The devil will tell you, "Play again, you will win", and you will end up losing everything. You may even keep gambling until you have lost all your possessions.

When these things are happening to you, you must learn the art of aggressive praying. Instead of praying a lot of people blame other things and leave the actual enemy alone.

When I was in the university, I used to feel sorry for some girls who spent all their money on clothes and make-up instead of feeding well enough. Since they denied their bodies the necessary food, they often ended up breaking down.

When a man brings out a biro and a piece of paper to calculate what his wife bought from the market, there is no point in the woman fighting him, he needs deliverance from the spirit of poverty.

THE STAND OF THE SCRIPTURES ON THE BAD KIND OF POVERTY

Let us read the stand of God on the bad kind of poverty.

Ecclesiastes 6:1-2 reads:

"There is an evil which I have seen under the sun, and it is common among men: A man to whom God hath given riches, wealth, and honour, so that he wanteth nothing for his soul of all that he desireth, yet God giveth him not power to eat thereof, but a stranger eateth it: this is vanity, and it is an evil disease."

The man has money but no power to eat thereof.

We know the story of Rockefeller, the American billionaire. There was a time in his life when all he could eat was milk and cracker-biscuit. The money he had was useless to him. It was the spirit of poverty that tormented him.

In Isaiah 65:22, we read:

"They shall not build, and another inhabit; they shall not plant, and another eat: for as the days of a tree are the days of my people, and mine elect shall long enjoy the work of their hands."

15

So, not enjoying the fruits of one's labour is caused by the spirit of poverty.

God warned the children of Israel against disobedience. He told them that if they disobeyed Him, the spirit of poverty would be released upon them.

In Deuteronomy 28:30-31, God curses whoever disobeyes Him. He says,

"Thou shalt betroth a wife, and another man shall lie with her: thou shalt build an house, and thou shalt not dwell therein: thou shalt plant a vineyard, and shalt not gather the grapes thereof. Thine ox shall be slain before thine eyes, and thou shalt not eat thereof: thine ass shall be violently taken away from before thy face, and shall not be restored to thee: thy sheep shall be given unto thine enemies, and thou shalt have none to rescue them."

Verse 33 says,

"The fruit of thy land, and all thy labours, shall a nation which thou knowest not eat up; and thou shalt be only oppressed and crushed alway:"

Verse 38 says,

"Thou shalt carry much seed out into the field, and shalt gather but little in; for the locust shall consume it."

Verse 40 says,

"Thou shalt have olive trees throughout all thy coasts, but thou shalt not anoint thyself with the oil; for thine olive shall cast his fruit."

Verses 43-44 reads,

"The stranger that is within thee shall get up above thee very high; and thou shalt come down very low. He shall lend to thee, and thou shalt not lend to him: he shall be the head, and thou shalt be the tail."

The spirit of poverty manifests in various ways and can even lead to sickness or death.

If you as a believer take no action, then nothing good will happen to you.

CURSE OF POVERTY

Some families are under a definite curse and each member is affected. When they get to the point of making it, something goes wrong, everything falls apart, and no one really gets anywhere. *Until that curse of poverty is broken, the spirit of poverty will remain in operation*. Any member of that family struggling to make it will just die, like a weak flame before a strong wind. But believers who are in this situation can do something about it.

Some jobs are under a curse and until you break that curse, the spirit will continue in operation.

Sometimes when a person is wrongfully dismissed from a company he will, out of bitterness, curse the company and this can put the company in trouble.

When bloody money is used to start a business, the business will be in trouble.

If the owner of a company, like the Chairman or the Managing Director, keeps harassing his female staff sexually, and they give in because they don't want to be sacked, the curse of poverty will

17

immediately come upon the man and his company. The evil emptier spirit will carry all his money to the demonic world.

Curses can be broken today, if you will repent and do something about it. Things would change for the better in your life.

BURIED POTENTIALS

The blackman has a special problem. We lock up or bury our potentials ourselves. The problem with many people is buried potentials.

One of the principles of success in life is to identify our God-given potentials and use them. The spirit of poverty has blinded many people and is therefore stealing their potentials.

Your God-given potential may be in your voice, memory, ability to organize things, business acumen, ability to understand and speak languages, analytical mind, ability to convince others, musical talent, powerful brain or foresight.

Identification and development of these potentials are essential for a successful life. Unfortunately, the potentials of many have been caged, giving room to the spirit of poverty to operate.

Those buried potentials must be exhumed today, in Jesus' name.

The spirit of poverty has used many parents against their children. A boy may begin to build a house with clay at an early age, and the unwary parent may keep warning the boy to stop it, thereby killing the boy's potential. Many parents warn their female children never to think of doing a job which they consider meant for men alone. If a child draws pictures, he or she is warned to stop doing an unserious job. The devil has deceived many parents to

18

believe that there are only three honourable professions, which are Medicine, Law and Engineering. This erroneous belief has planted the seed of the spirit of poverty in some families.

GATEWAYS TO POVERTY

The Bible, as a very kind book, shows us the gateways to poverty. They are:

1. STINGINESS

Proverbs 11:24-25 reads:

"There is that scattereth, and yet increaseth; and there is that withholdeth more than is meet, but it tendeth to poverty. The liberal soul shall be made fat: and he that watereth shall be watered also himself."

So, if you are stingy, you need to pray to be delivered, because it is a gateway to poverty.

2. LOVERS OF SLEEP AND SLUMBER

Proverbs 20:13 says,

"Love not sleep, lest thou come to poverty; open thine eyes, and thou shalt be satisfied with bread."

If you need an alarm-clock to wake you up, then you really need to pray.

19

3. FOLLOWING VAIN PERSONS

Proverbs 28:19 says,

"He that tilleth his land shall have plenty of bread: but he that followeth after vain persons shall have poverty enough."

Following vain persons leads to poverty.

4. LAZINESS

Proverbs 10:4:

"He becometh poor that dealeth with a slack hand: but the hand of the diligent maketh rich."

5. MOCKING THE POOR

Proverbs 17:5 says,

"Whoso mocketh the poor reproacheth his Maker: and he that is glad at calamities shall not be unpunished."

6. FAILURE IN PAYMENT OF TITHES AND OFFERING

Malachi 3:8-12:

"Will a man rob God? Yet ye have robbed me. But ye say, Wherein have we robbed thee? In tithes and offerings. Ye are cursed with a curse: for ye have robbed me, even this whole nation. Bring ye all the tithes into the storehouse, that there may be meat in mine house, and prove me now herewith, saith the LORD of hosts, if I will not open you the windows of heaven, and pour you out a blessing, that there shall not be room enough to receive it. And I will rebuke the devourer for your sakes, and he shall not destroy the fruits of your ground; neither shall your vine cast her fruit before the time in the field, saith the LORD of hosts. And all nations shall call you blessed: for ye shall be a delightsome land, saith the LORD of hosts."

Failure to pay tithes or to give offerings is the surest way to poverty.

7. NOT CONTRIBUTING TO GOD'S WORK

Haggai 1:6-8 explains this clearly:

"Ye have sown much, and bring in little; ye eat, but ye have not enough; ye drink, but ye are not filled with drink; ye clothe you, but there is none warm; and he that earneth wages earneth wages to put it into a bag with holes. Thus saith the LORD of hosts; Consider your ways. Go up to the mountain, and bring wood, and build the house; and I will take pleasure in it, and I will be glorified, saith the LORD."

8. GIVING TO GOD IN SMALL MEASURES

Luke 6:38 says,

"Give, and it shall be given unto you; good measure, pressed down, and shaken together, and running over, shall men give into your bosom. For with the same measure that ye mete withal it shall be measured to you again."

Remember this always, that with the same measure that you give, it shall be given to you.

9. ENGAGING IN THE WRONG BUSINESS

You'll find examples of this in the word of God. Luke 5: 1-10 is a good example:

"And it came to pass, that, as the people pressed upon him to hear the word of God, he stood by the lake of Gennesaret, And saw two ships standing by the lake: but the fishermen were gone out of them, and were washing their nets. And he entered into one of the ships, which was Simon's, and prayed him that he would thrust out a little from the land. And he sat down, and taught the people out of the ship. Now when he had left speaking, he said unto Simon, Launch out into the deep, and let down your nets for a draught. And Simon answering said unto him, Master, we have toiled all the night, and have taken nothing: nevertheless at thy word I will let down the net. And when they had this done, they inclosed a great multitude of fishes: and their net brake. And they beckoned unto their partners, which were in the other ship, that they should come and help them. And they came, and filled both the ships, so that they began to sink. When Simon Peter saw it, he fell down at Jesus' knees, saying, Depart from me; for I am a sinful man, O Lord. For he was astonished, and all that were with him, at the draught of the fishes which they had taken: And so was also James, and John, the sons of Zebedee, which were partners with Simon. And Jesus said unto Simon, Fear not; from henceforth thou shalt catch men."

10. NOT CARING FOR MEN OF GOD

Matthew 10: 35-42 says:

"For I am come to set a man at variance against his father,

and the daughter against her mother, and the daughter-in-law against her mother-in-law. And a man's foes shall be they of his own household. He that loveth father or mother more than me is not worthy of me: and he that loveth son or daughter more than me is not worthy of me. And he that taketh not his cross, and followeth after me, is not worthy of me. He that findeth his life shall lose it: and he that loseth his life for my sake shall find it. He that receiveth you receiveth me, and he that receiveth me receiveth him that sent me. He that receiveth a prophet in the name of a prophet shall receive a prophet's reward; and he that receiveth a righteous man in the name of a righteous man shall receive a righteous man's reward. And whosoever shall give to drink unto one of these little ones a cup of cold water only in the name of a disciple, verily I say unto you, he shall in no wise lose his reward."

11. NOT GIVING TO THE POOR

You'll find that in Proverbs 28:27.

"He that giveth unto the poor shall not lack: but he that hideth his eyes shall have many a curse."

12. THE CURSE OF POVERTY

Galatians 3:13 says:

"Christ hath redeemed us from the curse of the law, being made a curse for us: for it is written, Cursed is every one that hangeth on a tree:"

The curse of the law is three-fold- POVERTY, DISEASE AND

DEATH. Christ came to redeem us from all these.

13. IGNORANCE

Hosea 4:6 says:

"My people are destroyed for lack of knowledge: because thou hast rejected knowledge, I will also reject thee, that thou shalt be no priest to me: seeing thou hast forgotten the law of thy God, I will also forget thy children."

Ignorance regarding God's provision, of keys to success and prosperity, is a major cause of failure.

14. PRIDE

Out of pride, some people say they cannot do certain kinds of job. They feel they are too big to do any manual labour. For instance, they look the kind of job they feel is suitable for university graduates and so go about without any job. This is why many university graduates are employed by illiterate rich men today.

Such people feel it is below their dignity to start a business in a small way.

15. OSTENTATION

This is close to pride. Very high taste for expensive things and showing off. For example, buying the most expensive clothes, shoes, etc. Display of wealth, skill, etc. to obtain admiration or envy.

16. RIGIDITY

Refusal to change.

17. DISCOURAGEMENT

Giving up too soon, once the first attempt fails. Discouraged people believe they will fail, even before they start. They have programmed their minds towards failure. They are always expecting failure and they will fail. They will tell people that they knew all along that they were going to fail.

18. LACK OF GOOD COUNSELING

Refusal to seek spiritual counsel will lead to trouble and failure.

19. ENGAGING IN SECRET SIN

Sin hinders progress and hinders God's blessing too.

20. DEMONIC ACTIVITIES

These are the major forces responsible for failure, poverty and poor performances in our environment. They are the one that instigate thieves to burgle the businesses and houses of believers. They also chase away customers, cause fire outbreaks to destroy goods, and make debtors to refuse to pay.

21. WICKEDNESS

Job 15:20 says,

"The wicked man travaileth with pain all his days, and the number of years is hidden to the oppressor."

Job 15:23 says,

"He wandereth abroad for bread, saying, Where is it? he knoweth that the day of darkness is ready at his hand."

22. DISOBEDIENCE

Deut 28:15 reads:

"But it shall come to pass, if thou wilt not hearken unto the voice of the LORD thy God, to observe to do all his commandments and his statutes which I command thee this day; that all these curses shall come upon thee, and overtake thee:"

Deut 28:48 reads,

"Therefore shalt thou serve thine enemies which the LORD shall send against thee, in hunger, and in thirst, and in nakedness, and in want of all things: and he shall put a yoke of iron upon thy neck, until he have destroyed thee."

Prices are paid for disobedience.

23. LOVE OF PLEASURE

Prov 21:17 says,

"He that loveth pleasure shall be a poor man: he that loveth wine and oil shall not be rich."

THE SECRETS OF PROSPERITY

Prosperity is the state of being successful.

This means

- To be financially blessed by God.
- The ability to meet your needs and those of your dependants and to be able to assist others.
- Having no difficulty in meeting the needs and obligations of the home, church and society, etc.

Blessing is connected with life and curse is connected with death. Death and curses are in agreement. Life and blessings are in agreement.

True Bible prosperity is:

- To enjoy life and blessings.
- The ability of the Holy Spirit to make you to enjoy blessings and life.
- *The ability and knowledge to use God's power to meet your needs*.
- Having enough provision from God to carry out His plans for your life.

Let us look closely at a few scriptures.

Prov 10:15:

27

"The rich man's wealth is his strong city: the destruction of the poor is their poverty."

Prov 14:20:

"The poor is hated even of his own neighbour: but the rich hath many friends."

Eccl 5:19:

"Every man also to whom God hath given riches and wealth, and hath given him power to eat thereof, and to take his portion, and to rejoice in his labour; this is the gift of God."

3 Jn 1:2:

"Beloved, I wish above all things that thou mayest prosper and be in health, even as thy soul prospereth."

Phil 4:19:

"But my God shall supply all your need according to his riches in glory by Christ Jesus."

Matt. 6:33:

"But seek ye first the kingdom of God, and his righteousness; and all these things shall be added unto you."

2Chr. 1:12:

"Wisdom and knowledge is granted unto thee; and I will give thee riches, and wealth, and honour, such as none of the kings have had that have been before thee, neither shall there any after thee have the like."

Deut 8:18:

"But thou shalt remember the LORD thy God: for it is he that giveth thee power to get wealth, that he may establish his covenant which he sware unto thy fathers, as it is this day."

Beloved, wretchedness is not a blessing from God. Abraham, Joseph and Daniel were not poor.

Note these important truths.

- God is the source of prosperity.
- God is the author of prosperity. He made the earth and planted gold, minerals, oil, etc., in it.
- Every true child of God should reject poverty, strive and pray to be prosperous.
- Poverty is not a requirement for pleasing God, or entering heaven.
- Poverty is a prison.
- Poverty is a curse.
- There is a demon whose name is poverty.
- You can be the richest man and go to heaven. You can also be the poorest man and go to hell fire.
- There is what we call the anointing of poverty. Immediately anyone with that anointing enters into a place, even if the place was prospering before, poverty also enters.

Believers are more entitled to the good things of life than unbelievers and God's enemies.

The major problem we are having is that God cannot trust some of us with His money. Can God trust you with His riches?

Are you sufficiently broken to the point where you will not

backslide, no matter how rich you become?

Perhaps instead of crying to God to make you rich, you should first of all cry to be broken. Then He will bless you to a dumbfounding degree.

Money righteously acquired is not a sin, but the love of money is a sin.

Prosperity will not hinder your spiritual growth if you are truly broken.

Who do you think will grow faster in Christianity?

- The Christian who does not have transport money to attend meetings?

- Or, the christian who can afford to buy books, tapes and messages?

Wealth can help you to serve God better. Prosperous believers who finance church projects, help the church to grow faster than a person who wants to give but does not have.

KINDS OF PROSPERITY

There are three kinds of prosperity in the Bible.

1. Material prosperity

2. Spiritual prosperity

3. Prosperity in health

Many of us think that prosperity is only material. That is, not being poor and not wearing rags. No! Prosperity without good health is not worth anything. If you have billions of naira, but have an incurable disease, you are a pauper. God also wants you to prosper in health.

Read the following story:

One of Leo Tolstoi's most powerful short stories is entitled "How Much Land Does a Man Need?" The hero of this story is Pakhom, a small farmer with one basic grievance - he has very small piece of land.

One day, he learns of a new settlement beyond the Volga where one can buy as much land as one has money to pay, so he decides to seek his fortune in this new place. Gradually, he acquires land and more land, but not enough to satisfy him.

Then he hears that in the country of the Bashkirs, there is vast area of land available at a cheap price. He leaves his family at home and with his servant travels 300 miles to investigate. Soon after reaching the Bashkir camp, Pakhom enters into negotiations with the Bashkir chief.

"What is your price for the land?" Pakhom asks.

"Only a thousand rubles per day," the chief answers.

"How many acres would that include?" Pakhorn inquires, for he does not understand this day's rate at all.

"We do not reckon in that way," says the chief. "We sell only by the day. That is to say, as much land as you can walk around in a day, that much land is yours. That is our measure, and the price is a thousand rubles."

"Why," Pakhom says in an astonished voice, "a man might walk round a great deal in a day."

"He might indeed," the chief says, "but let me warn you about one thing. If on that same day you do not return to the spot where you

31

started, you lose your thousand rubles."

"It's a deal," says Pakhom, whose mind is made up to mark out a very large area of land the next day.

Before sunrise the next day Pakhom, his servant and the Bashkir chief with some of his men go to a hill overlooking a vast area of grassland. There the chief takes off his cap, lays it down, and says, "This will be the mark. Lay your money in it and have your servant remain beside it while you are gone. From this mark you will start and to this mark you will return."

Pakhom takes out his money, lays it in the cap, and then takes off. "I will walk toward the rising sun," he decides.

No sooner does the sun send its first rays across the horizon than Pakhom starts walking into the steppe, a couple of mounted Bashkir men riding behind him to plant stakes wherever Pakhom decides to have them. After a couple of miles Pakhom became warm and begins shedding some of his clothes. Later, when it really gets hot, he takes off his long boots. "Walking without them will be easier," he tells himself. On and on he walks far beyond the point where he should have turned north, but the farther east he goes the better the land becomes. He begins to tire now. Glancing at the sun he sees that it is time for lunch. He eats some bread but without sitting down. "Once I sit down, I'm likely to lie down and fall asleep."

He goes on again. At first he finds walking easy, for the meal has revived his strength. But soon the sun seems to grow all the hotter. Pakhom is almost worn out now, but keeps telling himself: "An hour's pain may be a century's gain." As he is about to head west he spots an excellent piece of land. "It would be a pity to leave that out," he thinks, so he continues north for a while.

It's getting late now and Pakhom has to be back before sunset.

So he finally heads south. "I must head straight back now, otherwise I won't make it back in time." His feet are aching badly. From time to time he staggers. There is such a long way to go yet. Pakhom pulls himself together and breaks into a run. On and on he runs. Now he can hear the Bashkirs cheering him on. He can see the cap and the chief sitting beside it. Pakhom reaches the hill just as the large red sun touches the earth. He scrambles up the slope. Then he stumbles and falls. While falling he stretches out his hand toward the cap and touches it.

"Ah, young man," the chief cries, "you have earned much land indeed!"

Pakhom does not hear, for when his servant tries to raise him up he finds that he is dead.

After a while the chief gets up, takes a spade from the ground, throws it to Pakhom's servant, and says, "Bury him!" (Culled from 'The God of Weakness' by J. Timmer.)

After the Bashkirs have left, the servant buries his master in a small plot of land just big enough for his body.

This man acquired more and more land, but was not satisfied. This man had land, but his spiritual poverty destroyed him.

What good is it to have wealth and go to hell fire? What good is it to have material prosperity and loose eternity?

God wants you to have prosperity in your spirit man, as well as in your health and material things.

He wants you to have good health. He wants you to fast, not because you have nothing to eat. Fasting due to lack of food does not bring fruits.

33

There is nothing more frustrating in life than being a lesser person than God wants you to be.

THE SOURCE OF PROSPERITY

Now, where does prosperity begin?

The inner-man.

When the inner-man prospers, the prosperity extends to the outside; that is, it radiates to the body and the environment.

What then are the secrets of the true Bible prosperity?

1. Get broken in every department of your life. Then God can trust you with His riches.

2. Know the causes of poverty and avoid them prayerfully.

3. Know the enemies of prosperity and avoid them.

4. Give generously to God. Do not take God's share. See Prov. 3:8-10, Malachi 3:10-12 and Luke 6:38.

5. Pray to prosper. Psalm 118:25 says,

"Save now, I beseech thee, O LORD: O LORD, I beseech thee, send now prosperity."

6. Strive as much as possible never to be a borrower or a debtor. Rom. 13:8 says,

"Owe no man any thing, but to love one another: for he that loveth another hath fulfilled the law."

Prov 22:7 also says:

"The rich ruleth over the poor, and the borrower is servant

to the lender."

7. Do not forget your source, that is, God. Ungratefulness will bring poverty.

8. Pursue holiness and spiritual prosperity.

9. Invest prayerfully and wisely. *Your best investment is always the gospel.* Mark 10:29-30 says,

"And Jesus answered and said, Verily I say unto you, There is no man that hath left house, or brethren, or sisters, or father, or mother, or wife, or children, or lands, for my sake, and the gospel's, But he shall receive an hundredfold now in this time, houses, and brethren, and sisters, and mothers, and children, and lands, with persecutions; and in the world to come eternal life."

Today is your day of powerful breakthroughs. If you have decisions to make, or sins to repent from, start doing this now, so that you can break the evil stronghold of poverty in your life.

God is not bothered with global economic situations. What He is interested in is that in whatever environment He has placed you, you must be a blessed person. It doesn't matter whether things are difficult in that environment or not. Even if there are problems around, as a child of God, you must not be a partaker.

The Lord is ready to reach out to you today, but you must first attract His attention. Heaven is ready to open up to you, if you bombard it with your prayers. Remember that God is not the author of evil. The person to fight is the devil and not God, your tenants, your colleagues or family members.

With every aggression in your spirit, pray the following prayer points:

1. O Lord, locate and revive all my buried potentials.

2. I break the curse of poverty in my life, in the mighty name of Jesus.

3. Spirit of poverty, I rebuke you and I bind you, in the name of Jesus.

4. Every spirit drinking the blood of my blessing, I bind you in the name of Jesus.

5. I smash the head of poverty on a wall of fire, in the name of Jesus.

6. Legs of poverty, walk out of my life now, in the name of Jesus.

7. Yoke of poverty, be broken, in the name of Jesus.

8. Let every garment of poverty in my life receive the fire of God, in the name of Jesus.

9. I reject financial burial, in the name of Jesus.

10. Let every satanic deposit be drained out of my business and handiwork, in the name of Jesus.

11. Let all the strange hands and legs begin to walk out of my business and handiwork, in the name of Jesus.

12. Let the spirit of favour baptise my business and handiwork, in the name of Jesus.

13. O Lord, enlarge my coast.

14. I rebuke every devourer in my finances, in the name of Jesus.

15. O Lord, cause ministering angels to bring in customers and money to me.

16. I bind every spirit of error upon my finances, in the name of Jesus.

17. O Lord, surprise me with abundance in my finances.

18. I bind every spirit of fake and unprofitable investments, in the name of Jesus.

19. Let the anointing for money-yielding ideas fall upon my life now, in the name of Jesus.

20. I command every strange money affecting my business to be neutralised by the blood of Jesus.

21. From now on, I refuse to wear the garment of debt, in the name of Jesus.

CHAPTER TWO

WEALTH MUST
CHANGE HANDS

INTRODUCTION

Deut 8:18: "But thou shalt remember the LORD thy God: for it is he that giveth thee power to get wealth, that he may establish his covenant which he sware unto thy fathers, as it is this day."

Ps 24:1: "The earth is the LORD's, and the fulness thereof; the world, and they that dwell therein."

Ps 34:10: "The young lions do lack, and suffer hunger: but they that seek the LORD shall not want any good thing."

Prov 8:18: "Riches and honour are with me; yea, durabie riches and righteousness."

It is time for believers to arise and possess their possessions. If we do not do so, we would allow unrestrained manifestations and operations of the enemy. Perhaps your labour has been going to Pharaoh and you have been paying your tithes to Egypt. Perhaps you have been struggling with the strugglers and wrestling with the wrestlers, it is time to arise and shake off the satanic dust. It is time for wealth to change hands from the hands of the oppressors to the hands of the children of God.

SPIRITUAL FORCE BEHIND MONEY

There is a spiritual force behind money and the unbelievers understand this very well. This is why they will do all in their power to get it.

Money, like air and water, is a necessity for life. It carries a lot of heavy loads. Take a dirty ₦10 note, look at it very well, it represents blood and toil. It is frightening because it can serve or destroy man.

Only God knows the secret of how many hands the money has passed through. Only God knows the good or evil that single note has done from the moment it was printed to its dirty ugly state now.

The money will not speak, it will never tell all it hides. It may be stained with sweat and blood. It is heavy with the weight of human toil. Many people might have died for it. Many people might have killed themselves for it, just to posses it for a few hours, to have a little pleasure, life and joy.

Only the Lord knows through how many hands it has passed and what it has done in the course of its long silent trip. It might have bought a wedding ring for a lover; paid for a baptismal card; fed a growing baby; bought food for a family; paid hospital bills; bought books for education; clothed people. At the same time, it might have sent a letter of breaking an engagement; paid for the death of a child in her mother's womb; bought alcohol to create a drunkard; produced films unfit for children; recorded indecent songs; bought the body of a woman for a few hours; paid for weapons of crime and the wood of a coffin.

This is why we believers should always pray on our money. We can pray like this:

"Lord, I thank You for the joy and the life this money has given. I ask You to clean my lot away from every evil it has done. I offer it back to You, Lord."

This is the secret behind the power of Mammon to trap people.

The most solid reason for the poverty of many Christians is their being stingy towards God, holding on too tight to money, thereby getting captured by Mammon. Loose yourself from the grip of money now.

God is not against His people having money. But He does not want money to have us. Money is neither good nor evil. A bad man's money will do bad things. A good man's money will do good things. Also, a bad man's money will be used for the kingdom of satan and a good man's money will be used for the kingdom of God. If you do not control money in accordance with God's will, it will kill you and leave your soul in hell.

WEALTH MUST CHANGE HANDS

Exod 3:22 says:

"But every woman shall borrow of her neighbour, and of her that sojourneth in her house, jewels of silver, and jewels of gold, and raiment: and ye shall put them upon your sons, and upon your daughters; and ye shall spoil the Egyptians."

II Ki 7:1-20:

"Then Elisha said, Hear ye the word of the LORD; Thus saith the LORD, To morrow about this time shall a measure of fine flour be sold for a shekel, and two measures of barley for a shekel, in the gate of Samaria. Then a lord on whose hand the king leaned answered the man of God, and said, Behold, if the LORD would make windows in heaven, might this thing be? And he said, Behold, thou shalt see it with thine eyes, but shalt not eat thereof. And there were four leprous men at the entering in of the gate: and they said one to another, Why sit we here until we die? If we say, We will enter into the city, then the famine is in the city, and we shall die there: and if we sit still here, we die also. Now therefore come, and let us fall unto the host of the Syrians: if they save us alive, we shall live; and if they kill us, we shall but die. And they rose up in the twilight, to go unto the camp of the Syrians: and when they were come to the uttermost part of the camp of Syria, behold, there was no man there. For the Lord had made the host of the Syrians to hear a noise of chariots, and a noise of horses, even the noise of a great host: and they said one to another, Lo, the king of Israel hath hired against us the kings of the Hittites, and the kings of the Egyptians, to come upon us. Wherefore they arose and fled in the twilight, and left their tents, and their horses, and their asses, even the camp as it was, and fled for their life. And when these lepers came to the uttermost part of the camp, they went into one tent, and did eat and drink, and carried thence silver, and gold, and raiment, and went and hid it; and came again, and entered into another tent, and carried thence also, and went and hid it. Then they said one to another, We do not well: this day is a day of good tidings, and we hold our peace: if we tarry till the morning light, some mischief will come upon us: now therefore come, that we may go and tell the king's household. So they came and called unto the porter of the city: and they told them, saying, We came to the camp of the Syrians, and, behold, there was no man there, neither voice of man, but horses tied, and asses tied, and the tents as they were. And he called the porters; and they told it to the king's house within. And the king arose in the night, and said unto his servants, I will now shew you what the Syrians have done to us. They know that we be hungry; therefore are they gone out of the camp to hide themselves in the field, saying, When they come out of the city, we shall catch them alive, and get into the city. And one of his servants answered and said, Let some take, I pray thee, five of the horses that remain, which are left in the city, (behold, they are as all the multitude of Israel that are left in it: behold, I say, they are even as all the multitude of the Israelites that are consumed:) and let us send and see. They took therefore two chariot horses; and the king sent after the host of the Syrians, saying, Go and see. And they went after them unto Jordan: and, lo, all the way was full of garments and vessels, which the Syrians had cast away in their haste. And the messengers returned, and told the king. And the people went out, and spoiled the tents of the Syrians. So a measure of fine flour was sold for a shekel, and two measures of barley for a shekel, according to the word of the LORD. And the king appointed the lord on whose hand he leaned to have the charge of the gate: and the people trode upon him in the gate, and he died, as the man of God had said, who spake when the king came down to him. And it came to pass as the man of God had spoken to the king, saying, Two measures of barley for a shekel, and a measure of fine flour for a shekel, shall be to morrow about this time in the gate of Samaria: And that lord answered the man of God, and said, Now, behold, if the LORD should make windows in heaven, might such a thing be? And he said, Behold, thou shalt see it with thine eyes, but shalt not eat thereof. And so it fell out unto him: for the people trode upon him in the gate, and he died."

Prov 13:22:

"A good man leaveth an inheritance to his children's children: and the wealth of the sinner is laid up for the just."

Isa 61:6:

"But ye shall be named the Priests of the LORD: men shall call you the Ministers of our God: ye shall eat the riches of the Gentiles, and in their glory shall ye boast yourselves."

Wealth must change hands! Power must change hands! Riches must change hands!

43

As believers, we must take charge of the wealth of the nations. Why? We all call God our Father in heaven.

A bad father allows his children to go hungry without clothes; he is lazy and does not spend on food and clothes for the family; never plays with members of the family and does not take notice of them; never punishes his children when they are wrong, lets them do what they like, etc. A good father is the opposite of all these.

God is a good father. God cares for us; He is interested in us; listens to us; and helps us to overcome difficulties of life. This same God owns the earth and the fullness thereof and we are His children. All the money in the world belongs to our heavenly Father.

Phil 4:19:

"But my God shall supply all your need according to his riches in glory by Christ Jesus."

Beloved, the sinners are laying up their riches for us to take over. It is the will of God to give us the riches of the gentiles.

Luke 18:29-30: **"And he said unto them, Verily I say unto you, There is no man that hath left house, or parents, or brethren, or wife, or children, for the kingdom of God's sake, Who shall not receive manifold more in this present time, and in the world to come life everlasting."**

If we allow the wealth to remain in the wrong hands, the preaching of the gospel will be hindered.

Prov 10:15: **"The rich man's wealth is his strong city: the destruction of the poor is their poverty."**

Money makes the slave a king and makes the junior to become the senior. At this point, open your mouth wide and make these two

44

proclamations:

I bind every spirit that creates scarcity in the midst of plenty, in the name of Jesus.

I refuse to be comfortable with poverty, in the name of Jesus.

STRATEGIES TO TAKE OVER THE WEALTH OF THE NATIONS

1. HOLINESS UNTO THE LORD

It is good to preach prosperity, but we must preach the message of holiness with prosperity.

Ps 37:25:

"I have been young, and now am old; yet have I not seen the righteous forsaken, nor his seed begging bread."

The condition for avoiding poverty is that we must live holy.

Matt 6:33:

"But seek ye first the kingdom of God, and his righteousness; and all these things shall be added unto you."

Prosperity is an automatic addition to your life after the issue of holiness has been sorted out. If you do not want to live holy and you are running after riches, the riches will kill you. God cannot trust you with His riches when your life is not in line with heaven.

2. HAVE THE RIGHT ATTITUDE TOWARDS MONEY

Rom 12:1-2:

"I beseech you therefore, brethren, by the mercies of God, that ye present your bodies a living sacrifice, holy, acceptable unto God, which is your reasonable service. And be not conformed to this world: but be ye transformed by the renewing of your mind, that ye may prove what is that good, and acceptable, and perfect, will of God."

Your consecration to the Lord is the basic requirement for any spiritual service. Have you presented your body to the Lord? Sacrifices have no power over the priest. We cannot sacrifice money to the Lord and His work, if we are not sacrificed.

Matt 27:5:

"And he cast down the pieces of silver in the temple, and departed, and went and hanged himself."

That money Judas received to betray Jesus was useless to him, but he discovered it too late.

Luke 16:13-16:

"No servant can serve two masters: for either he will hate the one, and love the other; or else he will hold to the one, and despise the other. Ye cannot serve God and mammon. And the Pharisees also, who were covetous, heard all these things: and they derided him. And he said unto them, Ye are they which justify yourselves before men; but God knoweth your hearts: for that which is highly esteemed among men is abomination in the sight of God. The law and the prophets were until John: since that time the kingdom of God is preached, and every man presseth into it."

In the passage above, Mammon is personified and treated as an idol, as a god. The word "cannot" means that we are unable to do so.

46

It is possible to work for two masters, but you can serve only one. You cannot carry a tree on both shoulders.

Mammon is the demon-power in control of money. It is the devil's salesman. He sells charms, spirits such as witchcraft, fame, etc. Mammon is the one responsible for distributing spirits of poverty to attack the human race, particularly Christians. He controls the demons of greed, selfishness, poverty and financial bankruptcy. Be determined in your spirit, even as you are reading this book, to defeat Mammon in your life and to bind his power and his demon spirits.

Mammon is an evil, spiritual power that grips men and enslaves them through money. It is the spiritual power that works in the world and in the lives of millions of people through their attitude towards money. You cannot serve God and Mammon. Not that you are despising money, but you are despising the satanic force that enslaves men and women through money. There is no neutrality. We must acknowledge in our lives the claim of one of them, God or Mammon.

Your attitude toward money reveals your attitude towards God. The person who tries to master Mammon by acquiring it would find that he has been captured.

Your attitude to money is very important and has to be examined. It is the love of money and inordinate love of money that will make you pick the money you find lying on the ground. It makes you to be ready at all cost to tell all forms of lie in order to obtain money. Paul describes the love of money as the "root of all evil."

1 Tim 6:10:

"For the love of money is the root of all evil: which while some coveted after, they have erred from the faith, and pierced

47

themselves through with many sorrows."

The love of money is capable of appearing as both good and evil at the same time. You have to have it; you have to keep it; you have to spend it; you have to share it. You either rule money or money rules you, whether you are poor or rich. Poverty does not free one from the rulership of money.

The inordinate love of money will turn both poor and rich men to thieves and tight-fisted sinners. You must dominate money or it will degrade you.

It is also the love of money that will make drivers to have accidents, make people drink terrible concoctions that lead to short life that turn people to murderers. The absence of money would have resulted in long life for many people. Many people are engaged in the accumulation of money thereby forgetting their souls. Some people run businesses on Sundays. Many married women will commit adultery to raise money.

Money of affliction and sin will only lead to more problems. Such money will remove good money from you, it will spoil the lives of the children you used it to train. This is why the Bible talks about restitution:

Lev 6:1-4:

"And the LORD spake unto Moses, saying, If a soul sin, and commit a trespass against the LORD, and lie unto his neighbour in that which was delivered him to keep, or in fellowship, or in a thing taken away by violence, or hath deceived his neighbour; Or have found that which was lost, and lieth concerning it, and sweareth falsely; in any of all these that a man doeth, sinning therein: Then it shall be, because he hath sinned, and is guilty, that he shall restore that which he took violently away, or the thing which he hath deceitfully gotten, or that which was delivered him to keep, or the lost thing which he found,"

Hab 2:6:

"Shall not all these take up a parable against him, and a taunting proverb against him, and say, Woe to him that increaseth that which is not his! how long? and to him that ladeth himself with thick clay!"

How to know if you have the love of money

- **Exaggerated importance.** When losing money is to you like losing your person. When losing money or its absence will lead to depression, or an attempt to commit suicide, then you have the love of money.

- **Over-estimation of the power of money.** Wealthy people who think there is nothing money cannot do because they have the love of money will be shocked to discover that there are things that money cannot purchase. Poor people use to imagine that anything can be bought with money. This is not true. Money will buy bed, but not sleep; it will buy books, but not brain; it will buy medicine, but not health; it will buy amusement, but not happiness; it will buy church pews, but not heaven.

- **It controls actions.** When as a result of money you are bowing to unscriptural circumstances, you have the love of money. True riches are spiritual and they involve our being conformed to the image of God's Son.

Beloved, has your money been delivered from self and the world? If you are controlling your money or the world is controlling it, then you have not submitted yourself to God completely.

49

Have you turned God into a rubbish heap? Some people give what they do not need.

Do you give only what you cannot feel? If so, then you are making God to be a beggar.

This world has been judged.

Matt 6:19-21: "Lay not up for yourselves treasures upon earth, where moth and rust doth corrupt, and where thieves break through and steal: But lay up for yourselves treasures in heaven, where neither moth nor rust doth corrupt, and where thieves do not break through nor steal: For where your treasure. is, there will your heart be also."

This is a serious matter for the believer. We cannot keep our money here, we will lose it. Look at some banks that are distressed now, can you keep money in them? The world is just as bankrupt. You must bank in heaven.

The money that God will need to finish His work on earth has been in the world before you were born. God will not force you to part with your money.

It has been discovered that many people do not know God's key to prosperity. Luke 6:38 tells us the key. It says:

"Give, and it shall be given unto you; good measure, pressed down, and shaken together, and running over, shall men give into your bosom. For with the same measure that ye mete withal it shall be measured to you again."

Look at the case of King Solomon. He built a great temple to the Lord;

I King 6:2-3:

"And the house which king Solomon built for the LORD, the length thereof was threescore cubits, and the breadth thereof twenty cubits, and the height thereof thirty cubits. And the porch before the temple of the house, twenty cubits was the length thereof, according to the breadth of the house; and ten cubits was the breadth thereof before the house."

I King 7:12:

"And the great court round about was with three rows of hewed stones, and a row of cedar beams, both for the inner court of the house of the LORD, and for the porch of the house."

However many people mistakenly think that giving is a matter for the rich alone. This is proved wrong in Mark 12:43-44:

"And he called unto him his disciples, and saith unto them, Verily I say unto you, That this poor widow hath cast more in, than all they which have cast into the treasury: For all they did cast in of their abundance; but she of her want did cast in all that she had, even all her living."

This woman gave all she had. She was in desperate need, but she gave all. Has your money been delivered from self and the world? Some turn God into a rubbish heap - they give what they do not need. Others give only what they cannot feel.

Money has strong power to imprison its owners and divert their love from Jesus.

- Do you love money?

- Do you inwardly crave for money?

- Are you dissatisfied because of money?

51

- Do you go worrying about to make more money?

If your answers are yes, you should seek for deliverance or perish.

Every believer is responsible before God for what he supports or promotes. God loves cheerful givers. He has no rooms for those who are pressurized into giving. Many pastors are in the business of pressurizing people into giving. This is an abomination. They receive 4 or 5 offerings in one service.

Matt 6:1-4 says:

"Take heed that ye do not your alms before men, to be seen of them: otherwise ye have no reward of your Father which is in heaven. Therefore when thou doest thine alms, do not sound a trumpet before thee, as the hypocrites do in the synagogues and in the streets, that they may have glory of men. Verily I say unto you, They have their reward. But when thou doest alms, let not thy left hand know what thy right hand doeth: That thine alms may be in secret: and thy Father which seeth in secret himself shall reward thee openly."

Believers should work hard and make money, but must invest the money in God's work.

1Thes 3:7-12:

"Therefore, brethren, we were comforted over you in all our affliction and distress by your faith: For now we live, if ye stand fast in the Lord. For what thanks can we render to God again for you, for all the joy wherewith we joy for your sakes before our God; Night and day praying exceedingly that we might see your face, and might perfect that which is lacking in your faith? Now God himself and our Father, and our Lord Jesus Christ, direct our way unto you. And the Lord make you to increase and abound in love one toward another, and toward all men, even as we do toward you:"

The Consequences of not giving to the Lord

There are consequences of not giving to the Lord or not giving enough.

- You will not be given spiritual riches.

Not giving to the Lord is dishonesty. It is unfaithfulness over things that must pass away.

Luke 16:10-12:

"He that is faithful in that which is least is faithful also in much: and he that is unjust in the least is unjust also in much. If therefore ye have not been faithful in the unrighteous mammon, who will commit to your trust the true riches? And if ye have not been faithful in that which is another man's, who shall give you that which is your own?"

The Lord has given them to us to find out if we can handle them for Him. If we do not give them back to God, we are saying that the riches of heaven cannot be entrusted to us.

- What we keep will not be a blessing to us.

Hag 1:4-11:

"Is it time for you, O ye, to dwell in your cieled houses, and this house lie waste? Now therefore thus saith the LORD of hosts; Consider your ways. Ye have sown much, and bring in little; ye eat, but ye have not enough; ye drink, but ye are not

filled with drink; ye clothe you, but there is none warm; and he that earneth wages earneth wages to put it into a bag with holes. Thus saith the LORD of hosts; Consider your ways. Go up to the mountain, and bring wood, and build the house; and I will take pleasure in it, and I will be glorified, saith the LORD. Ye looked for much, and, lo, it came to little; and when ye brought it home, I did blow upon it. Why? saith the LORD of hosts. Because of mine house that is waste, and ye run every man unto his own house. Therefore the heaven over you is stayed from dew, and the earth is stayed from her fruit. And I called for a drought upon the land, and upon the mountains, and upon the corn, and upon the new wine, and upon the oil, and upon that which the ground bringeth forth, and upon men, and upon cattle, and upon all the labour of the hands."

The Lord says the same thing today. When believers fail to give, problems will start. This explains the following situations:

- Increasing droughts and floods
- Diminishing resources of God's children
- Increased salary but still broke.

Nothing works well until you repent and give God His due

- You are cursed with a curse

Mal 3:8-9:

"Will a man rob God? Yet ye have robbed me. But ye say, Wherein have we robbed thee? In tithes and offerings. Ye are cursed with a curse: for ye have robbed me, even this whole nation."

We cannot bless whom God has cursed. Imagine you, a believer,

54

being a thief. When God curses people, they can no longer make spiritual progress. They cannot receive revelation from the Lord. They become barren in many ways. The spiritual malady of many God's children may be traced to the fact that they stole from God.

There is a way out. Repentance and restitution. Lift the curse by paying back what you have stolen.

You must remember that only believers can give to God's work and expect rewards.

Prov 15:8:

"The sacrifice of the wicked is an abomination to the LORD: but the prayer of the upright is his delight."

- Do you have large sums of money stored in the bank? Invest some in the bank of heaven. Did the Lord ask you to lock such a large sum away?

- Do you have lands, farms, houses, etc? Have you prayed about the possibility of selling some and investing the money in bank of heaven?

- Do you have expensive jewelleries? Sell them and transfer the money to heaven.

If you cannot give enough to the Lord, may be it is time you stopped buying soft drinks, coffee, etc.

- Have you totally given your life to the Lord? Your money is the indication.

Listen to this life story.

As a young man, John D. Rockefeller, Sr., was as strong and husky as a farm lad. When he entered business he drove himself harder than any slave was ever driven by the whip of a taskmaster. At the early age of 33, he had made his first million dollars. By consecrating every waking moment to his work, he controlled, at 43, the biggest business in the world. When he was 53, he was the richest man on earth and the world's only billionaire.

For this achievement he had bartered his own happiness and health. He developed alopecia, a condition in which not only the hair of the head drops off but also most of the hair from the eyelashes and eyebrows. One of his biographers said that he looked like a "mummy." His weekly income was a million dollars, but his digestion was so bad that he could eat only crackers and milk.

Like Scrooge, John D. was as solitary as an oyster. He once confessed that he "wanted to be loved," but did not sense that people love only those who emanate affection. Lacking in consideration for others, he had often crushed the helpless into the mire in his lust to make bigger profits. So hated was he in the oil fields of Pennsylvania that the men whom he had pauperized hanged him in effigy, and he had bodyguards day and night. The mass of wealth he had accumulated gave him neither peace nor happiness. In fact, as he sought to protect and control it, he discovered that he was being smothered by it. He could not sleep; he enjoyed nothing.

When John D. was only 53, Ida Tarbell wrote of him, "An awful age was in his face. He was the oldest man that I have ever seen." The crackers and milk he glumly swallowed could no longer hold together his skinny body and restless soul. It was generally agreed that he would not live another year, and newspaper writers had his obituary written and ready in the files.

Then John D. began to do some thinking in the long nights when he couldn't sleep. One night he made a startling discovery: *he would*

56

not to take even one of his thin dimes with him into the next world!
His was a despair and helplessness of the little boy who sees the
relentless tide coming in to sweep into oblivion all the sand castles
he has been building.

For the first time in his life he recognized that money was not a
commodity to be hoarded but something to be shared for the benefit
of others. In the morning he, like Scrooge, lost no time in
transforming his money into blessings to others. He began to help
worthy causes. He established the Rockefeller Foundation so that
some of his fortune could be channeled to needed areas. It would
require a book to describe the benefits that resulted from the many
hundreds of millions of dollars that he showered on universities,
hospitals, mission work, and millions of underprivileged people. He
was the one who helped rid the South of its greatest economic and
physical scourge - hookworm. We can thank John D. every time our
lives and the lives of our children are saved by an injection of
penicillin because his contributions aided in the discovery of this
miracle drug. His money sparked the research that saved and is still
saving millions of people from untimely deaths from malaria,
tuberculosis, diphtheria and many other diseases.

It is not my purpose to detail the blessings the world received
when John D. changed the current of his thinking from *getting* to
giving. My object is to tell you that when he began to think *outwardly*
toward the needs of others, a miracle occurred. He began to sleep,
to eat normally, and to enjoy life in general. The bitterness, rancor
and the deadness of self-centeredness went out of his life, and into
his soul came refreshing streams of love and gratitude from those
whom he was helping. He who had been repulsive and lifeless now
seethed with vibrancy and activity.

When Rockefeller was 53, it certainly appeared that he would never celebrate another birthday, but he started to practice one of God's eternal laws, and he reaped his promised benefits: ". . . give, **and it shall be given unto you: good measure, pressed down, shaken together, running over, shall give into your bossom.**" He proved the fulfilment of this promise for he lived not only to celebrate his 54th and 55th birthdays, but experienced "the good measure . . . running over" - he lived up to 98. (Culled from 'None of these diseases' by S. I. McMillen.)

3. HATE POVERTY WITH PERFECT HATRED

You have to make up your mind that poverty is not your lot. Decide to be an enemy of poverty.

4. WORK HARD

Prov 24:33-34:

"Yet a little sleep, a little slumber, a little folding of the hands to sleep: So shall thy poverty come as one that travelleth; and thy want as an armed man."

Prov 12:11:

"He that tilleth his land shall be satisfied with bread: but he that followeth vain persons is void of understanding."

Prov 22:29:

"Seest thou a man diligent in his business? he shall stand before kings; he shall not stand before mean men."

Christians are not to be lazy. The Bible is against laziness and lack of diligence. It is sad, but it is true that many believers are plain lazy. You must put hard work into whatever you are doing. You must burn the mid-night oil. You must study hard.

5. TITHE FAITHFULLY

Always ensure that you pay your tithes correctly in order to open the windows of heaven on your life. (Mal. 3:8-10).

6. CHANGE YOUR OFFERINGS

You must be faithful in giving your offerings as commanded by the Scriptures. Take a decision that you will increase your offerings with immediate effect. Change your offerings and change your destiny.

7. PRAY POVERTY-DESTROYING AND WEALTH-RELEASING PRAYERS REGULARLY.

Examples of these can be found at the back of this book.

8. DETERMINE TO INVEST IN THE KINGDOM OF GOD.

PRAYER WARFARE SECTION

HOW TO PRAY RESULT-ORIENTED PRAYERS

It is strongly advised that you pray in any of these ways as led by the Holy Spirit:

A. 7 days' night vigil (praying from 12 midnight to 3:00 a.m.).

B. 7 days' fast daily (breaking at 7:00 p.m.).

C. 21 days' night vigil (praying from 12 midnight to 3:00 a.m.).

D. 21 days' fast daily (breaking at 7:00 p.m.).

E. 3 or more days of dry fast.

Note: All prayers must be said very aggressively (not mumbled) in the name of Jesus.

NUMBER 1 - WEALTH MUST CHANGE HANDS

Scripture reading: 2Kings 7

Confession: Deut. 8:18

Praise Worship

1. I withdraw my wealth from the hand of the bondwoman and her children, in the name of Jesus.

2. I will not squander my divine opportunities, in the name of Jesus.

3. I must pray to get results in this programme, in the name of Jesus.

4. I dismantle any power working against my efficiency, in the name of Jesus.

5. I refuse to lock the door of blessings against myself, in the name

of Jesus.

6. I refuse to be a wandering star, in the name of Jesus.

7. I refuse to appear to disappear, in the name of Jesus.

8. Let the riches of the Gentiles be transferred to me, in the name of Jesus.

9. Let the angels of the Lord pursue every enemy of my prosperity to destruction, in the name of Jesus.

10. Let the sword of the Goliath of poverty turn against it, in the name of Jesus.

11. Let wealth change hands in my life, in the name of Jesus.

12. O Lord, make a hole in the roof for me for my prosperity.

13. Let the yoke of poverty upon my life be dashed to pieces, in the name of Jesus,

14. Let every satanic siren scaring away my helpers be silenced, in the name of Jesus,

15. Let every masquerading power swallowing my prosperity be destroyed, in the name of Jesus.

16. Let every coffin constructed against my prosperity swallow the owner, in the name of Jesus.

17. Let the ways of the angels of poverty delegated against me be dark and slippery, in the name of Jesus.

18. Lord Jesus, hold my purse.

19. Every demonic scarcity, be dissolved by fire, in the name of Jesus.

20. By the wealthy name of Jesus, let heavenly resources rush to my door.

21. I attack my lack with the sword of fire, in the name of Jesus.

22. Satanic debt and credit, be dissolved, in the name of Jesus.

23. Oh Lord, be my eternal cashier.

24. I bind the spirit of debt. I shall not borrow to eat, in the name of Jesus.

25. Every evil meeting summoned against my prosperity, scatter without repair, in the name of Jesus.

26. Every arrow of wickedness fired against my prosperity, be disgraced, in the name of Jesus.

27. Let my life magnetize favour for breakthroughs, in the name of Jesus.

28. I arrest every gadget of poverty, in the name of Jesus.

29. I recover my blessings from any body of water, forest and satanic banks, in the name of Jesus.

30. Let all my departed glory be restored, in the name of Jesus.

31. Let all my departed virtues be restored, in the name of Jesus.

32. Let God arise and let all my stubborn pursuers scatter, in the name of Jesus.

33. Every attack by evil night creatures, be disgraced, in the name of Jesus.

34. Let the wings of every spirit flying against me be dashed to pieces, in the name of Jesus.

35. Angels of the living God, search the land of the living and the land of the dead and recover my stolen properties, in the name of Jesus.

36. Every gadget of frustration, be dashed to pieces, in the name of

Jesus.

37. I break every curse of poverty working upon my life, in the name of Jesus.

38. I bind every spirit drinking the blood of my prosperity, in the name of Jesus.

39. O Lord, create new and profitable opportunities for me.

40. Let ministry angels bring customers and favour to me, in the name of Jesus.

41. Anyone occupying my seat of prosperity, clear away, in the name of Jesus.

42. Lord, make a way for me in the land of the living.

43. I bind the spirit of fake and useless investment, in the name of Jesus.

44. All unsold materials, be sold with profit, in the name of Jesus.

45. Let all business failures be converted to success, in the name of Jesus.

46. Every curse on my hands and legs, be broken, in the name of Jesus.

47. O Lord, embarrass me with abundance in every area of my life.

48. Every strange money affecting my prosperity, be neutralized, in the name of Jesus.

49. Let brassy heavens break forth and bring rain, in the name of Jesus.

50. I break the control of every spirit of poverty over my life, in the name of Jesus.

51. Lord Jesus, anoint my eyes to see the hidden riches of this

world.

52. Lord Jesus, advertise Your breakthroughs in my life.

53. Let the riches of the ungodly be transferred into my hands, in the name of Jesus.

54. I will rise above the unbelievers around me, in the name of Jesus.

55. O Lord, make me a reference point of divine blessings.

56. Let blessings invade my life, in the name of Jesus.

57. Let the anointing of excellence fall on me, in the name of Jesus.

58. I disarm Satan king and authority over my prosperity, in the name of Jesus.

59. Let harvest meet harvest in my life, in the name of Jesus.

60. Let harvest overtake the sower in my life, in the name of Jesus.

61. Every curse pronounced against my source of income, be broken, in the name of Jesus.

62. Let my breakthroughs turn around for good, in the name of Jesus.

63. Curses working against my destiny, break, in the name of Jesus.

64. O Lord, network me with divine helpers.

65. Let life-transforming breakthroughs overtake me, in the name of Jesus.

66. Let divine ability overtake me, in the name of Jesus.

67. O Lord, lead me to those who will bless me.

68. Let my favour frustrate the plant of the enemy, in the name of Jesus.

69. I will witness the downfall of my strongman, in the name of Jesus.

70. I will be a lender and not a borrower, in the name of Jesus.

71. My labour shall not be in vain, in the name of Jesus.

72. Let the blessings which there will be no room to receive overtake me, in the name of Jesus.

73. O Lord, plant me by the rivers of prosperity.

74. Unknown evil seeds in my life, I command you to refuse to germinate, in the name of Jesus.

75. I refuse to get stuck on one level of blessing, in the name of Jesus.

76. I shall posses all the good things I pursue, in the name of Jesus.

77. Every effect of cursed house and land upon my prosperity, break, in the name of Jesus.

78. Every power shielding me away from breakthrcughs, fall down and die, in the name of Jesus.

79. Let the garden of my life yield super abundance, in the name of Jesus.

80. Every desert spirit, loose your hold upon my life, in the name of Jesus.

81. Holy Spirit, plug my life into divine prosperity, in the name of Jesus.

82. Every Achan in the camp of my breakthroughs, be exposed and be disgraced, in the name of Jesus.

83. Every power operating demonic gadget against my prosperity, fall down and die, in the name of Jesus.

84. Every power passing evil current into my finances, lose your hold, in the name of Jesus.

85. I break every cycle of financial turbulence, in the name of Jesus.

86. I smash the head of poverty on the wall of fire, in the name of Jesus.

87. Ugly feet of poverty, walk out of my life now, in the name of Jesus.

88. Let every garment of poverty receive the fire of God, in the name of Jesus.

89. I reject financial burial, in the name of Jesus.

90. Let every garment of poverty receive the fire of God, in the name of Jesus.

91. I reject financial burial, in the name of Jesus.

92. I reject every witchcraft burial, in the name of Jesus.

93. Woe unto every vessel of poverty pursuing me, in the name of Jesus.

94. Let the fire of God burn away evil spiritual properties, in the name of Jesus.

95. Poverty-identification marks, be rubbed off by the blood of Jesus.

96. O Lord, heal every financial leprosy in my life.

97. Let my foundation be strengthened to carry divine prosperity, in the name of Jesus.

98. Every stolen and satanically transferred virtues, be restored, in the name of Jesus.

99. Let every ordination of debt over my life be canceled, in the

name of Jesus.

100. O Lord, create newer and profitable opportunities for me.

101. Every strange fire ignited against my prosperity, be quenched, in the name of Jesus.

102. Let those sending my money to spiritual mortuary fall down and die, in the name of Jesus.

103. Every power scaring away my prosperity, be paralysed, in the name of Jesus.

104. Every familiar spirit sharing my money before I receive it, be bound permanently, in the name of Jesus.

105. Let every inherited design of poverty melt away by fire, in the name of Jesus.

106. Let every evil re-arrangement of prosperity be dismantled, in the name of Jesus.

107. Lead me, O Lord, to my own land that flows with milk and honey.

108. Let satanic giants occupying my promised land fall down and die, in the name of Jesus.

109. O Lord, empower me to climb my mountain of prosperity.

110. Strongman of poverty in my life, fall down and die, in the name of Jesus.

111. Spirits of famine and hunger, my life is not your candidate, in the name of Jesus.

112. I remove my name from the book of financial embarrassment, in the name of Jesus.

113. Every power reinforcing poverty against me, loose your hold, in the name of Jesus.

114. I release myself from every bondage of poverty, in the name of Jesus.

115. The riches of the gentiles shall come to me, in the name of Jesus.

116. Let divine magnet of prosperity be planted in my hands, in the name of Jesus.

117. I retrieve my purse from the hand of Judas, in the name of Jesus.

118. Let there be a reverse transfer of my satanically transferred wealth, in the name of Jesus.

119. I take over the wealth of the sinner, in the name of Jesus.

120. I recover the steering wheel of my wealth from the hand of evil drivers, in the name of Jesus.

121. I refuse to lock the door of blessings against myself, in the name of Jesus.

122. O Lord, revive my blessings.

123. O Lord, return my stolen blessings.

124. O Lord, send God's angels to bring me blessings.

125. O Lord, let everything that needs change in my life to bring me blessings be changed.

126. O Lord, uncover to me my key for prosperity.

127. Every power sitting on my wealth, fall down and die, in the name of Jesus.

128. O Lord, transfer the wealth of Laban to my Jacob.

129. Let all those who hate my prosperity be put to shame, in the name of Jesus.

130. Every evil bird swallowing my money, fall down and die, in the name of Jesus.

131. Every arrow of poverty, go back to where you came from, in the name of Jesus.

132. I bind every word spoken against my breakthroughs, in the name of Jesus.

133. Every business house energised by satan, fold up, in the name of Jesus.

134. I destroy every clock and timetable of poverty, in the name of Jesus.

135. Every water spirit, touch not my prosperity, in the name of Jesus.

136. Let men and women rush wealth to my doors, in the name of Jesus.

137. I reject temporary blessings, in the name of Jesus.

138. Every arrow of poverty energised by polygamy, fall down and die, in the name of Jesus.

139. Every arrow of poverty energised by household wickedness, fall down and die, in the name of Jesus.

140. Let power change hands in my finances, in the name of Jesus.

141. Let every serpent and scorpion of poverty die, in the name of Jesus.

142. I refuse to eat the bread of sorrow. I reject the water of affliction, in the name of Jesus.

143. Let divine explosion fall upon my breakthroughs, in the name of Jesus.

144. The enemy will not drag my finances on the ground, in the

name of Jesus.

145. O Lord, advertize Your wealth and power in my life, in the name of Jesus.

146. Let promotion meet promotion in my life, in the name of Jesus.

147. I pursue and overtake my enemies and recover my wealth from them, in the name of Jesus.

148. Holy Spirit, direct my hands into prosperity, in the name of Jesus.

NUMBER 2 - PRAYERS FOR PROFITABLE SALES

Confessions: Ps.46:1; Heb. 1:14; Phil. 4:19; Num 6:25; Det. 28:13; Dan.1:17; Ps. 5:12; 119:165

Praise Worship

1. Father, I dedicate and consecrate these products to You, in the name of Jesus.

2. Lord, bless the efforts of all who are involved in selling my products.

3. Lord, give my people favour with the customers.

4. Father, help my salesmen to understand the needs of my customers.

5. Lord, help my sales representative never to oversell, but always to efficiently present my products and services.

6. Father, let the Holy Spirit teach me sales promotion and increasing sales techniques.

7. Lord, help me to always remain ahead and not behind.

8. Lord, help me to offer my products in the proper way.

9. Lord, give my salesmen favour when making sales.

10. Almighty Father, cause a hunger or request for my goods and services, in the name of Jesus.

11. Lord, open new doors and provide new markets for my goods and services.

12. Lord, help me to increase sales and add new products daily.

13. I retrieve my products from every evil attack, in Jesus' name.

14. I break every curse of failure upon the sales of my products, in the name of Jesus.

15. I command the devil to take off his legs from my goods and services, in the name of Jesus.

16. Let the rod of iron fall on any strange money passed to me, in the name of Jesus.

17. I use the Blood of Jesus Christ to wash my hands and my products and make them clean today, in the name of Jesus.

18. Let there be breakthroughs for me in my transactions, in the name of Jesus.

19. Lord, let me have the spirit of favour in all my business transactions.

20. I ask for the release of prosperity on the sales of my products, in the name of Jesus.

21. Let all demonic hindrances to the sales of my products be totally paralysed, in the name of Jesus.

22. I break every circle of sales failure upon my products, in the name of Jesus.

23. Let my products be shielded from all evil observers, in the name of Jesus.

24. Father, let Your angels lift up my products on their hands so that they do not strike their feet against a stone, in Jesus' name.

25. I remove my products from the dominion of the powers of darkness, in the name of Jesus.

26. Let my products become a channel of blessings and a foundation of life for other businesses, in the name of Jesus.

27. I command my money being caged by the enemy to be completely released, in the name of Jesus.

28. Lord, give me supernatural breakthroughs in all my present

business proposals.

29. I bind and put to flight all the spirits of fear, anxiety and discouragement, in the name of Jesus.

30. Lord, let divine wisdom fall upon all who are supporting me in selling my products.

31. I break the backbone of any further spirits of conspiracy and treachery, in the name of Jesus.

32. Lord, hammer my matter into the mind of those who will assist me in selling my products so that they do not suffer from demonic loss of memory.

33. I paralyse the handiwork of household enemies and envious agents in selling my products, in the name of Jesus.

34. You devil, take your legs away from the top of my finances, in the mighty name of Jesus.

35. Let the fire of the Holy Spirit purge my finances from any evil mark put upon me, in the name of Jesus.

36. Father, guide and direct me to rectify any problem I have with my business.

37. Lord, forgive me for any wrong decision or action I have taken or any wrong thought.

38. Father, help me to see my mistakes and faults and to do all in my power to overcome and correct them, in the name of Jesus.

39. Lord, give unto me the Eagle eye and eyes of Elisha to foresee market situations.

40. Lord, give me wisdom to walk out of any unfavorable business situations.

41. Lord, always help me to identify evil business traps.

42. Lord, help me to erect safeguards to prevent business failure.

43. Lord, help me to be on the lookout for ways to provide better products and services.

44. In the mighty name of Jesus, I claim the following:

    (a) good reputation   (b) favour with clients and customers

    (c) abundant prosperity   (d) divine wisdom for those who occupy important decision-making positions

    (e) increased sales and services and expanded markets

    (f) new product ideas and new servicing concepts.

NUMBER 3 - UPROOTING THE TREE OF NON-ACHIEVEMENT

NOTE: Prayers of uprooting the tree of non-achievement have to be said aggressively and violently. No stone should be left unturned. You must hate the spirit of non-achievement with perfect hatred.

Confessions: Gal. 3:13-14; Matt. 3:11; Col. 1:13; 2:15; 2Tim. 4:18; Heb. 2:15; Psalm 27:2.

Praise worship

1. Thank God for making provision for deliverance from any form of bondage.

2. Confess your sins and those of your ancestors, especially those sins linked to evil powers.

3. I cover myself with the blood of Jesus.

4. I release myself from any inherited bondage, in Jesus' name.

5. O Lord, send Your axe of fire to the foundation of my life and destroy every evil plantation.

6. Let the blood of Jesus flush out from my system every inherited satanic deposit, in the name of Jesus.

7. I release myself from the grip of any problem transferred to my life from the womb, in the name of Jesus.

8. I break and loose myself from every inherited evil covenant, in the name of Jesus.

9. I break and loose myself from every inherited evil curse, in the name of Jesus.

10. I vomit every evil consumption that I have been fed with as a child, in the name of Jesus.

11. I command all foundational strongmen attached to my life to be paralysed, in the name of Jesus.

12. Let any rod of the wicked rising up against my family line be rendered impotent for my sake, in the name of Jesus.

13. I cancel the consequences of any evil local name attached to my person, in the name of Jesus.

14. You evil foundational plantations, come out of my life with all your roots, in the name of Jesus.

15. I break and loose myself from every form of demonic bewitchment, in the name of Jesus.

16. I release myself from every evil domination and control, in the name of Jesus.

17. Let every gate opened to the enemy by my foundation be closed forever with the blood of Jesus.

18. Lord Jesus, walk back into every second of my life and deliver me where I need deliverance, heal me where I need healing, transform me where I need transformation.

19. Let every evil imagination against me wither from the source, in the name of Jesus.

20. Those laughing me to scorn shall witness my testimony, in the name of Jesus.

21. Let the destructive plan of the enemies aimed against me blow up in their faces, in the name of Jesus.

22. Let my point of ridicule be converted to a source of miracle, in the name of Jesus.

23. Let all powers sponsoring evil decisions against me be disgraced, in the name of Jesus.

24. Let the stubborn strongman delegated against me fall down to the ground and become impotent, in the name of Jesus.

25. Let the stronghold of every spirit of Korah, Dathan and Abiram militating against me be smashed to pieces, in Jesus' name.

26. Let every spirit of Balaam hired to curse me fall after the order of Balaam, in the name of Jesus.

27. Let every spirit of Sanballat and Tobiah planning evil against me receive the stones of/fire, in the name of Jesus.

28. Let every spirit of Egypt fall after the order of Pharaoh, in the name of Jesus.

29. Let every spirit of Herod be disgraced, in the name of Jesus.

30. Let every spirit of Goliath receive the stones of fire, in the name of Jesus.

31. Let every spirit of Pharaoh fall into the Red Sea of their own making, in the name of Jesus.

32. Let all satanic manipulations aimed at changing my destiny be frustrated, in the name of Jesus.

33. Let all unprofitable broadcasters of my goodness be silenced, in the name of Jesus.

34. Let all leaking bags and pockets be sealed up, in Jesus' name.

35. Let all evil monitoring eyes fashioned against me be blind, in the name of Jesus.

36. Let every evil effect of strange touches be removed from my life, in the name of Jesus.

37. I command all demonic reverse gears installed to hinder my progress to be roasted, in the name of Jesus.

38. Any evil sleep undertaken to harm me should be converted to dead sleep, in the name of Jesus.

39. Let all weapons and devices of oppressors and tormentors be rendered impotent, in the name of Jesus.

40. Let the Fire of God destroy the power operating any spiritual vehicle working against me, in the name of Jesus.

41. Let all evil advice given against my favour crash and disintegrate, in the name of Jesus.

42. Let the wind, the sun and the moon run contrary to every demonic presence in my environment, in the name of Jesus.

43. You devourers, vanish from my labour, in the name of Jesus.

44. Let every tree planted by fear in my life dry up to the roots, in the name of Jesus.

45. I cancel all enchantments, curses and spells that are against me, in the name of Jesus.

46. Let all iron-like curses break, in the name of Jesus.

47. Let divine tongue of fire roast any evil tongue against me, in the name of Jesus.

77

NUMBER 4 - REMOVING BLOCKAGES OPERATING AT THE EDGE OF MIRACLES

Praise worship

1. I confess my sins of exhibiting occasional doubts.

2. Let the Angels of the living God roll away the stone blocking my financial, physical and spiritual breakthroughs, in the name of Jesus.

3. I bind every spirit manipulating my beneficiaries against me, in the name of Jesus.

4. I remove my name from the book of seers of goodness without appropriation, in the name of Jesus.

5. Let God arise and let all the enemies of my breakthrough be scattered, in the name of Jesus.

6. Let the Fire of God melt away the stones hindering my blessings, in the mighty name of Jesus.

7. Let the cloud blocking the sunlight of my glory and breakthrough be dispersed, in the name of Jesus.

8. All secrets of the enemy in the camp of my life that are still in the darkness, let them be revealed to me now, in Jesus' name.

9. All evil spirits masquerading to trouble me, be bound, in the name of Jesus.

10. Lord, let me not put unprofitable and heavy load upon myself, in the name of Jesus.

11. All keys to my goodness that are still in the possession of the enemy, Lord, give them unto me.

12. Open my eyes o Lord, and let my ways be not darkened before me.

13. All my sweat on the affairs of my life will not be in vain, in the name of Jesus.

14. The pregnancy of good things within me will not be aborted by any contrary power, in the name of Jesus.

15. Lord, turn me to untouchable coals of fire.

16. Lord, let wonderful changes begin to be my lot from this week.

17. Lord, remove covetousness from my eyes.

18. Lord, fill the cup of my life to the brim.

19. Let every power stepping on my goodness receive the arrow of the fire of God now, in the name of Jesus.

20. I reject every spirit of the tail in all areas of my life, in Jesus' name.

21. Thank God for the victory.

NUMBER 5 - VICTORY OVER FINANCIAL HANDICAP

Note:

1. Before you begin this prayer session, carry out a search of your spiritual life. Repent from all known sins, confess such sins to the Lord and ask for forgiveness.

2. Have you broken the laws of divine prosperity? For example, are you faithful in your giving tithe and offerings? Have you ever used your money to sponsor evil? E.g. ., abortion, demonic consultation, sacrifice to idols and demons? Have you been stingy when you had money? Are you guilty of abandoning your marital and family responsibilities?

3. After sorting out all these things with the Lord, embark on seven (7) days prayers and fasting using the under listed prayer

points.

Confessions: Phil. 4:19; Psalm 23:6; Deut. 8:8; 3John 2; Psalm 84:11; Psalm 24; Phil. 4:13.

Praise worship

1. I command all demonic hindrances to my prosperity to be totally paralyzed, in the name of Jesus.

2. Let every demonic bank keeping my finances be destroyed and release my finances, in the name of Jesus.

3. I bind every strongman holding my finances captive, in the name of Jesus.

4. I possess all my possession, in the name of Jesus.

5. I break and loose myself from every curse of financial bondage and poverty, in the name of Jesus.

6. I release myself from every conscious and unconscious covenant with the spirit of poverty, in the name of Jesus.

7. Let Cod arise and let every enemy of my financial breakthrough be scattered, in the name of Jesus.

8. O Lord, restore all my wasted years and efforts and convert them to blessings, in the name of Jesus.

9. Let the spirit of favour be upon me every where I go concerning my finances, in the name of Jesus.

10. Father, I ask You, in the name of Jesus, to send ministering spirits to bring in prosperity and funds into my finances.

11. Let men bless me anywhere I go, in the name of Jesus.

12. I release my finances from the clutches of financial hunger, in the name of Jesus.

13. I loose angels, in the mighty name of Jesus, to go and create favour for my finances.

14. Let all financial hindrances be removed, in the name of Jesus.

15. I remove my name and those of my customers from the book of financial bankruptcy, in the name of Jesus.

16. Holy Spirit, be my senior partner in my finances.

17. Every good thing presently eluding my finances should flow into them, in the mighty name of Jesus.

18. I reject every spirit of financial embarrassment, in Jesus' name.

19. Father, block every space causing unprofitable leakage to my finances, in the mighty name of Jesus.

20. Let my finances become too hot to handle for dupes and demonic customers, in the name of Jesus.

21. Let spiritual magnetic power that attracts and keeps wealth be deposited in my finances, in the name of Jesus.

22. I release my finances from the influences, control and domination of household wickedness, in the name of Jesus.

23. Let all satanic angels deflecting blessings away from me be completely paralyzed, in the name of Jesus.

24. Let the evil effect of any strange money I have ever received or touched be neutralised, in the name of Jesus.

25. O Lord, teach me the divine secret of prosperity.

26. Let the joy of the enemy on my financial life be converted to sorrow, in the name of Jesus.

27. Let all my blessings held captive locally or overseas be released to me, in the name of Jesus.

28. I bind every anti-breakthrough, anti-miracle and anti-prosperity forces, in the name of Jesus.

29. Let my finances be too hot for any evil power to sit upon, in the name of Jesus.

30. O Lord, quicken my spirit to evolve money-yielding ideas.

31. Let every spirit of debt and financial blockage be rendered impotent for my sake, in the name of Jesus.

32. O Lord, bring honey out of the rock for me and let me find the way where men say there is no way.

33. Thank the Lord for the answers.

NUMBER 6 - HONEY OUT OF THE ROCK

Confession - Deut. 28:13, Job 22:28, Ps. 8:5; 30:5; 73:24; 118:24, Prov. 21:1; 11:27, Dan. 1:9, Zech. 12:10, John 10:27, 1Cor. 4:5, Eph. 3:19-20; 5:17; 2Tim. 1:7.

Praise worship

1. Father, make all my proposals to find favour in the sight of . . . ·· in the name of Jesus.

2. Lord, let me find favour ,compassion and loving-kindness with . . . concerning this business.

3. Let all the demonic obstacles that have been established in the heart of . . . against my prosperity be destroyed, in the name of Jesus.

4. Lord, show . . . dreams, visions and restlessness that would advance my cause.

5. I command my money being caged by the enemy to be completely released, in the name of Jesus.

6. Lord , give me supernatural breakthroughs in all my present business proposals.

7. I bind and put to flight all the spirits of fear, anxiety and discouragement, in the name of Jesus.

8. Lord, let divine wisdom fall upon all who are supporting me in these matters.

9. I break the backbone of any further spirits of conspiracy and treachery, in the name of Jesus.

10. Lord, hammer my matter into the mind of those who will assist me so that they do not suffer from demonic loss of memory.

11. I paralyse the handiwork of household enemies and envious agents in this matter, in the name of Jesus.

12. You devil take your legs away from the top of my finances, in the mighty name of Jesus.

13. Let the fire of the Holy Spirit purge my finances from any evil mark put upon me, in the name of Jesus.

14. Father, guide and direct me to rectify any problem I have with my business.

15. Lord, forgive me for any wrong decision or action I took or any wrong thought.

16. Father, help me to see my mistakes and faults and to do all in my power to overcome and correct them, in the name of Jesus.

17. Father, show me what to do so that business crisis would not arise again in my business in the name of Jesus.

18. Lord, give unto me the eagle eye and eyes of Elisha to foresee market situations.

19. Lord, give us wisdom to walk out of any unfavorable business

situations.

20. Father, help me to formulate a plan of recovery to keep me at the top, in the name of Jesus.

21. Lord, send me divine counsellors who can help me with my business.

22. Lord, always help me to identify evil business traps.

23. Lord, help me to erect safeguards to prevent business failure.

24. Let Your seal and divine stamp fall upon all my business proposals, in the name of Jesus.

25. Let my proposals be too hot for the enemy to sit upon, in the name of Jesus.

26. Father, give us the anointing to get the job done above and beyond our own strength, abilities, gifts and talents.

27. Lord, help us to be on the lookout for ways to provide better products and services.

28. Lord, help me to yield to the Holy Spirit whenever I encounter circumstances beyond my knowledge.

29. In the mighty name of Jesus, I claim the following:
    (a) good reputation   (b) favour with clients and customers
    (c) abundant prosperity
    (d) divine wisdom for those who occupy important decision-making positions
    (e) increased sales and services and expanded markets
    (f) new product ideas and new servicing concepts

30. Lord, help me to do my very best at all times.

31. Father, I dedicate and consecrate my business to You, in the

name of Jesus.

32. Thank the Lord for answered prayers.

NUMBER 7 - FINDING FAVOUR WITH OTHERS

Confessions - Deut 28:13, Prov 21:1; 11:27, Zech 12:10, Ps 8:5, Eph 3:19-20, Ps 30:5, Dan 1:9

Praise worship

1. Father, make all my proposals to find favour in the sight of . . ., in the name of Jesus.

2. Lord, let me find favour, compassion and loving-kindness with . . . concerning this business.

3. Let all the demonic obstacles that have been established in the heart of . . . against my prosperity be destroyed, in the name of Jesus.

4. Lord, show . . . dreams, visions and restlessness that would advance my cause.

5. I command my money being caged by the enemy to be completely released, in the name of Jesus.

6. Lord , give me supernatural breakthroughs in all my present business proposals.

7. I bind and put to flight all the spirits of fear, anxiety and discouragement, in the name of Jesus.

8. Lord, let divine wisdom fall upon all who are supporting me in these matters.

9. I break the backbone of any further spirits of conspiracy and treachery, in the name of Jesus.

10. Lord, hammer my matter into the mind of those who will assist me so that they do not suffer from demonic loss of memory.

11. I paralyse the handiwork of house hold enemies and envious agents in this matter, in the name of Jesus.

12. You devil, take your legs away from the top of my finances, in the mighty name of Jesus.

13. Let the fire of the Holy spirit purge my life from any evil mark put upon me, in the name of Jesus.

14. Thank the Lord for answered prayers.

Books in this series

▸Power Against Spiritual Terrorists
▸Deliverance For The Head
▸The Great Deliverance
▸Power Against Coffin Spirits
▸Revoking Evil Decrees
▸Limiting God

To order for the tape of this message
write to or call at
MFM Tapes Ministry,
13, Olasimbo Street, Onike, Yaba,
☎ 01-868766 Lagos.

Other Publications By MFM Ministries
▸Students In The School Of Fear
▸The Vagabond Spirit
▸Power Must Change Hands
▸Breakthrough Prayers For Business Professionals
▸Pray Your Way To Breakthroughs (Third Edition)
▸Spiritual Warfare And The Home
▸Victory Over Satanic Dreams (Second Edition)
▸Personal Spiritual Check-Up
▸Prayers That Bring Miracles (In English, Hausa, Igbo & Yoruba Languages -
1996 Seventy Days Fasting Prayer)
▸"Adura Agbayori" (Yoruba version of the Second Edition of Pray Your Way To
Breakthroughs)
▸How To Obtain Personal Deliverance (Second Edition)
▸Power Against Local Wickedness
▸Brokenness
▸Let God Answer By Fire (1997 Seventy Days Fasting & Prayer Programme In
English, French, Hausa, Igbo and Yoruba Languages)
▸Release From Destructive Covenants

Mountain of Fire and Miracles Ministries, is a ministry devoted to the revival of Apostolic Signs, Holy Ghost Fireworks and the unlimited demonstration of the power of God to deliver to the uttermost.

Absolute holiness within and without, as the greatest spiritual insecticide, and a condition for Heaven is taught openly. MFM is a do-it-yourself Gospel Ministry, where your hands are trained to wage war and your fingers to fight.

* Sunday - Worship 7:00 a.m.
* Monday - Spiritual Hospital 5:30 p.m.
* Wednesday - MFM Revival Service 5:30 p.m.
* 1st Saturday of every month -
"Power Must Change Hands" 7:00 a.m.
* 3rd Saturday of every month -
Spinsters' & Bachelors' Meeting 7:00 a.m.
* 3rd Saturday of every month -
Business Fellowship - 10 a.m.

JESUS IS LORD!